Acrim

CW00969054

MICHAEL HOFMANN

Acrimony

faber and faber

LONDON · BOSTON

First published in 1986 by
Faber and Faber Limited
3 Queen Square London WC1N 3AU

Photoset by Wilmaset Birkenhead Wirral
Printed in Great Britain by
Redwood Burn Ltd Trowbridge Wiltshire
All rights reserved

British Library Cataloguing in Publication Data

Hofmann, Michael
Acrimony.
I. Title
821'.914   PR6058.01
ISBN 0–571–14527–2
ISBN 0–571–14528–0 Pbk

Library of Congress Cataloging-in-Publication Data

Hofmann, Michael, 1957–
Acrimony.
I. Title.
PR6058.0345A66 1986   821'.914   86–11546
ISBN 0–571–14527–2
ISBN 0–571–14528–0 (pbk.)

For my Father and Mother

Acknowledgements and thanks:

Blatant Acts of Poetry II, Firebird 3 (Penguin), *London Magazine, London Review of Books, New Statesman, Oxford Poetry, P.E.N. New Poetry 1* (Quartet), *PN Review, Poetry Book Society Christmas Supplement 1983, Poetry International, Poetry Now* (Radio 3), *Poetry Review, Some Contemporary Poets of Britain and Ireland* (Carcanet), *Times Literary Supplement*.

'My Father's House Has Many Mansions', 'Between Bed and Wastepaper Basket' and 'Entr'acte' won small prizes in the National Poetry Competitions of 1983, 1984 and 1985; 'Changes' was first published in the *New Yorker*; 'Vortex', 'Withdrawn from Circulation', 'Giro Account' and 'Old Firm' in the *Paris Review*; and 'Author, Author' (as 'Not Talking') in *Poetry*.

Thanks to Roy Foster for 'Kensal Rise' and for the artichoke to Charlie Hunt.

Man müsste so sich ineinanderlegen
wie Blütenblätter um die Staubgefässe:
so sehr ist überall das Ungemässe
und häuft sich an und stürzt sich uns entgegen.

                                                    Rilke

Contents

PART 1

PART 2: MY FATHER'S HOUSE

PART 1

Ancient Evenings

(for A.)

My friends hunted in packs, had themselves photographed
under hoardings that said 'Tender Vegetables'
or 'Big Chunks', but I had you – my Antonia!
Not for long, nor for a long time now . . .

Later, your jeans faded more completely,
and the hole in them wore to a furred square,
as it had to, but I remember my hands
skating over them, there where the cloth was thickest.

You were so quiet, it seemed like an invitation
to be disturbed, like Archimedes and the soldier,
like me, like the water displaced from my kettle
when I heated tins of viscous celery soup in it

until the glue dissolved and the labels crumbled
and the turbid, overheated water turned into more soup . . .
I was overheated, too. I could not trust my judgement.
The coffee I made in the dark was eight times too strong.

My humour was gravity, so I sat us both in an armchair
and toppled over backwards. I must have hoped
the experience of danger would cement our relationship.
Nothing was broken, and we made surprisingly little noise.

On the Margins

Hospitality and unease, weekend guests
in this Chekhovian rectory painted a frivolous
blush pink. It is comfortable and fallen,
as though run by children, but with an adult's
guiding hand for basics, food, warmth, light . . .
At other times, what conversations, what demeanours!
I stare at myself in the grey, oxidized mirror
over the fireplace, godless, inept, countrified.
The distance disappears between rooms and voices.
Stuffy and centripetal, I tag after my hosts,
talking, offering 'help', sitting on tables
or leaning ungraciously in the doorway.

We drove twenty miles to buy roses, to a stately home
behind a moat and a pair of netted Alsatians.
The shaggy, youthful master of the house
was already on to his second family. His little boy
must have guessed. He had the exemplary energy
of the late child, working on his parents' stamina,
boisterous and surexcited, running to fetch us
prayer books, one at a time, they were so heavy.

Back here, I feel again spiritless, unhappy, the wrong age.
Not to be condescended to, still less fit for equality.
I quarrel with you over your word 'accomplished',
and then slink off upstairs to make it up . . .
We hear the hoarse, see-saw cries of the donkeys
grazing in the churchyard, mother and daughter,
and the first mosquitoes bouncing up and down,
practising their verticals like a video game. Next door,
his green clothes hung on pegs, Eric, the rustic burr,
is taking a bath, whistling and crooning happily
in his timeless, folkloric voice. I pat your nakedness.
In evil whispers, I manage to convince you.

Changes

Birds singing in the rain, in the dawn chorus,
on power lines. Birds knocking on the lawn,
and poor mistaken worms answering them . . .

They take no thought for the morrow, not like you
in your new job. – It paid for my flowers, now
already stricken in years. The stiff cornflowers

bleach, their blue rinse grows out. The marigolds
develop a stoop and go bald, orange clowns,
straw polls, their petals coming out in fistfuls . . .

Hard to take you in your new professional pride –
a salary, place of work, colleagues, corporate spirit –
your new *femme d'affaires* haircut, hard as nails.

Say I must be repressive, afraid of castration,
loving the quest better than its fulfilment.
– What became of you, bright sparrow, featherhead?

Impotence

The dry electric heat of Cornwall turned us yellow
in a week . . . All that time, we didn't sweat
and I never touched you. Debility, cursed idleness,
I read slowly through my book of African stories.
The honeysuckle in the lanes came from some tropics,
and the strange, acidulous, blue-paper hydrangeas.
Farmers strung up crows as an example to others.
One afternoon, we lay down and slept in a warm mist.

That was our fourth summer. Afterwards, I went
to squat in your parents' house – hanging around alone
while you trooped off to family weddings, and came home
in a gaggle of tradition and collective enchantment.
Your father pedantically whistled a whole verse of a hymn,
and went down to the end of the garden to hide his tears.
We talked dictionaries, and he gave me his kindly
'Dutch uncle' spiel. ('Tell it to the Marines!')

Then his typewriter tapped out messages from the dead
as he pursued his genealogy. Distant, fish-jawed relations
from New Zealand came to stay, and Scottish cousins
so alike they were one prototype, a foursome of twins
ground out by the mills of marriage and proximity.
Most evenings, I was aphasic, incapable of speech,
worn down by tolerance and inclusion. My arms twitched
as though my shirt had been the shirt of Nessus . . .

Now it's October, I'm hawking and spitting in the rain.
The damp air puts out my cigarettes. All round me,
this London *faubourg* of service flats, gigolos, blackmail.
Gymnasial grunts echo from the Lego barracks:
the Voice of America, and a flag to brighten the dullest day.
The Marines, sombre and muscle-bound – shaved

                                          knuckleheads!
Over the road, the flat-topped studio, once a church,
with the spire taken off it. The employees kneel all week,

gearing up a car for its commercial début.
Its numberless licence plate proclaims the new ORION,
blinded by Merope's father, slaughtered by Artemis,
now up in television heaven . . . Some old wasps
drag from drainpipe to window, as if it didn't matter,
and your three wooden municipal garden seats are just

                                          anywhere
in your concrete garden, where by some providential freak
a wild strawberry plant is leaping about in the cracks.

Epithalamion

'The old couple, owners of this crabby, marine hotel,
sit in their armchairs like Canute, talking of

nothing but the circling death of their Great Dane.
Out on the terrace, the proud, demented peacocks

crack their breakfast eggs on cement. Our honeymoon,
seedy and British. Character to proficiency –

no shy, intrusive maid, bringing us champagne . . .
In church, ladies' hats outnumbered our friends.

We were the minister's "young friends". He told us
about love and called us "Richard and Stephen".

Were we the Princes in the Tower? The whole edifice
rested on us, on her stiff dress and my tie-pin.

No one could help us. With his shock of white hair
and his mangy dog-collar, the minister arraigned us,

yelping against the flesh like a dog in the manger,
importuned, blundering, resentful, exploited.

He thought he was performing a rescue service –
a fireman at midnight, two cats up a tree in flames . . .'

Cinders

The talking was over, so we listened to the rain
chattering on the roof. We were both derailed.
I watched the veins stand out on her throat
as she retold the gags of the Black comedian.

His face crisped and creased by a cocaine blowback,
he kidded about being on fire, running down the street . . .
My opportunist heart ticked, our sprawled limbs
on the sofa, my cigarettes, the old flames of her henna.

How could I sleep, when I knew that across the city
she was purifying herself in the manner of unhappy women,
all damage and despair, greedy for punishment,
hunting for split ends till five a.m.?

Friction

Resistance, the hum of ohms, the coiled wire
cries out in its vacuum, in the too-powerful bulb.

Our silence is irksome and confrontational.
As you sit across from me, I could wish you away:

turning the pages of a book, your pen grinding
on my paper – I quarrel with each manifestation.

Your new dress is in an older, plainer style,
belted but voluminous. It would double for pregnancy.

Asleep, motorized, tidal, you drive me to the wall.
Each cycle you complete is a waste of youth,

a chemical sadness. The time passes. Doesn't love
entail risks? We hope, pretend, take precautions.

Amplitude is for the future, it needs confidence.
I stay on home ground – cageyness, stasis, ennui –

but even that's untenable . . . When you left me again,
I took out a pipe-cleaner and caught a drop of tar

on its thin, fleecy tip –
                          as if that caused the impediment!

Ploughshares

My sheets rode from left to right. Soon I was lying
on the bare security mattress, my arm round a white wraith.
. . . I remembered the film I saw. Wizened and high-cheeked,
the tartar face of Adenauer, first post-war Chancellor,
elected with the margin of one vote, his own. That
was the 'Adenauer era' . . . He warned against Communism
'of the Asiatic type', and said that a free Europe
should extend to the Urals. Improbably, and by subterfuge,
he re-armed Germany (even Strauss, the young outside-right,
wanted 'the arm that held a weapon' to 'drop off'),
and, but for the opposition of the Göttingen professors
and great popular demonstrations, it would have gone nuclear
as well . . . In my dream, the peaceable objects in the larder
flew off, changed their function, their identity,
even, when it was safe to do so, their labels.

Going East

Anthracite and purges, the old upright carriages
of the *Deutsche Reichsbahn*, of old Imperial Germany . . .

Among the bird-cherries and ceramics factories
on both sides, the frontier is a moment of distinction.

The crossing-point is the good count Gutenfürst:
where Alsatians defend the Republic like Cerberus

protecting Hell, their leashes noosed to a wire –
vibrant, free-running, holding on like grim death.

Aerial Perspective

Where the picturesque collides with the strategically
important, in some dog-eared, dog-rose corner
of Cornwall or Suffolk, there's a clutch of airbases,
and a weekend cottage called Boeing's Rest . . .

I can only hear the big AWACS aircraft
homing back in the fog across the North Sea –
tailplanes like leg-nutcrackers, and ridden by
their great, rotating, white-striped black toadstools –

but no doubt they can see us blips, as they can see
the blind gophers chewing up the putting-surface,
and the discarded copy of *Pull* or *Weapon* lying in a hole
in the road: men at work, a reassuring sight.

A Floating City

After the card-players, the cuba libre drinkers
and the readers of two-day-old newspapers,
there are the night strollers, pastel shades down the
                                        bobble-lit
Atlantic esplanade, by the small roar of the waves.

We saw the passenger liner put in for the afternoon,
then put out again: a floating city, heading South,
then pulling a slow turn, end on to the shore,
and backing North-West for the Azores or the
                                        shipping-lanes –

a wide and wasteful curve, elegiac and deceptive,
like that of your plane (and its decoy), that I followed
standing in the jetstream as they lifted away,
penny-pinching Britannias on their chartered tails . . .

The place was demolished in an earthquake and rebuilt
on a new site: built down, having learned its lesson,
wide and flat, built for cars. – With you gone out of it,
it seems destroyed again, and rebuilt to less purpose.

I stand on Avenue Mohammed V like a crowd hoping for a
                                        motorcade.
When the King comes to stay, he's like an earthquake,
living with the one thing his paranoia can live with,
the migrant population he calls an entourage.

A Brief Occupation

(for Gilles)

Six floors up, I found myself like a suicide –
one night, the last thing in a bare room . . .
I was afraid I might frighten my neighbours,
two old ladies dying of terror, thinking
every man was the gasman, every gasman a killer . . .

I was not myself. I was just anyone. The next day,
the place was going to be sold. Every so often,
high-spirited car horns bypassed the dead-end street.
The outside wall was a slowly declining roof,
an electricity meter clung to life by a few threads . . .

There was an inhuman shortage of cloth in that room:
a crocheted rug with a few eloquent hairs on it,
a stone for a pillow, my coat hanging demurely in the
window.
The hairs belonged to a girl, now back in Greece,
an island, a museum of mankind.

Entr'acte

The enemies of democracy were back supporting it.
Soldiers went in fear of their MPs, looked slippy
on the parade ground, tumbling from their personnel carriers,
parleyed in groups of two and three with girls at the gate.

I sat and picnicked on my balcony, no picnic,
eyeing the tarmac through the rusty gridiron underfoot,
flicking ash and wincing at my pips going lickety-split,
hitting the deck fifty feet down, among the sentries . . .

Inside, the wall met neither floor nor ceiling.
Two stripes of light reached into my room from next door,
where I heard an American girl – mezzo, ardent –
crying, 'Don't come, sweet Jesus, not yet.'

In the Realm of the Senses

One perfunctory fuck on our first night,
then nothing for ever . . . only jokes and hard lines,
cold water, mushy soap and sleep that never comes.
We hurt with tiredness, and are abashed by our dirt.

We fall further behind the days, our overnighted systems
struggle with smoke and sights and *consommations*.
The yellow Citroën sits up and fills its lungs,
a black and white green-backed mongrel sees us off.

The road skirts the airport like a stray runway.
Incoming planes make as if to pick us off.
Sometimes it divides: one half runs along the ground,
the other makes a sudden hump – my fear of flyovers.

A little further, I read the simple-minded vertical lettering
on *Ariane*, the unmanned European rocket, the harmless beige
skin-tone of *café au lait*, falling back to earth
in eighty seconds, no use even to the weatherman . . .

We return late at night, my eyes are on stalks,
the breeze whips them into stiff peaks of inflammation
as they stare and stare at the city lights, *Gruppensex*,
Massage Bar, the breasts a woman bared to cool . . .

Our cat has sprayed the house to greet us.
Lust hurts him into eloquence, almost speech –
like the rabble-rousing live music on the record player,
cynical, manipulative, knowing where it wants to go.

Too tense for sex, too slow to kill, nothing
is as loud as the throbbing duet of the pigeons
in their bay on the roof, as the hours he spent
trapped in a thorn-bush, inhaling a local beauty.

Eclogue

Industry undressing in front of Agriculture –
not a pretty sight. The subject for one
of those allegorical Victorian sculptures.
An energetic mismatch. But Pluto's hell-holes
terminate in or around the flower-meadows
and orchards of Proserpine. Ceres's poor daughter
is whisked away by the top-hatted manufacturer
on his iron horse . . . Brick huts in the fields,
barred mine entrances from the last century,
narrow-gauge railways, powdery cement factories.
A quarry is an inverted cathedral: witchcraft,
a steeple of air sharpened and buried in the ground.
– All around these dangerous sites, sheep graze,
horned and bleating like eminent Victorians.

Nighthawks

(for James Lasdun)

Time isn't money, at our age, it's water.
You couldn't say we cupped our hands very tightly . . .
We missed the second-last train, and find ourselves
at the station with half an hour to kill.

The derelicts queue twice round the tearoom.
Outside, the controlled prostitutes move smoothly
through the shoals of men laughing off their fear.
The street-lamps are a dull coral, snakes' heads.

Earlier, I watched a couple over your shoulder.
She was thin, bone-chested, dressed in black lace,
her best feature vines of hair. Blatant, ravenous,
post-coital, they greased their fingers as they ate.

I met a dim acquaintance, a man with the manner
of a laughing-gas victim, rich, frightened and jovial.
Why doesn't everyone wear pink, he squeaked.
Only a couple of blocks are safe in his world.

Now we've arrived at this hamburger heaven,
a bright hole walled with mirrors where our faces show
pale and evacuated in the neon. We spoon our sundaes
from a metal dish. The chopped nuts are poison.

We've been six straight hours together, my friend,
sitting in a shroud of earnestness and misgiving.
Swarthy, big-lipped, suffering, tubercular,
your hollow darkness survives even in this place . . .

The branch-line is under the axe, but it still runs,
rattling and screeching, between the hospital
lit like a toy, and the castellated factory –
a *folie de grandeur* of late capitalism.

Albion Market

Warm air and no sun – the sky was like cardboard,
the same depthless no-colour as the pavements and buildings.
It was May, and pink cherry blossoms lay and shoaled
in the gutter, bleeding as after some wedding . . .

Broken glass, corrugated tin and spraygunned plywood
                                                    saying
Arsenal rules the world. Twenty floors up Chantry Point,
the grey diamond panels over two arsoned windows
were scorched like a couple of raised eyebrows.

Tireless and sick, women hunted for bargains.
Gold and silver were half-price. Clothes shops
started up, enjoyed a certain vogue, then
went into a tailspin of permanent sales,

cutting their throats. A window waved *Goodbye, Kilburn*,
and *Everything Must Go*. The *Last Day* was weeks ago –
it didn't. The tailor's became *Rock Bottom*.
On the pavement, men were selling shoelaces.

A few streets away, in the renovated precinct,
girls' names and numbers stood on every lamp-post,
phone-booth, parking meter and tree. Felt tip on sticky
                                                    labels,
'rubber', and 'correction' for the incorrigible.

At night, the taxis crawled through Bayswater,
where women dangled their 'most things considered' from
                                                    the kerb.
A man came down the street with the meth-pink eyes
of a white rat, his gait a mortal shuffle.

A British bulldog bowler hat clung to his melting skull.
. . . Game spirits, tat and service industries,
an economy stripped to the skin trade. Sex and security,
Arsenal boot boys, white slaves and the SAS.

From Kensal Rise to Heaven

Old Labour slogans, *Venceremos*, dates for demonstrations
like passed deadlines – they must be disappointed
to find they still exist. Halfway down the street,
a sign struggles to its feet and says Brent.

The surfaces are friable, broken and dirty, a skin unsuitable
for chemical treatment. Building, repair and demolition
go on simultaneously, indistinguishably. Change and decay.
– When change is arrested, what do you get?

The Sun, our Chinese takeaway, is being repainted.
I see an orange topcoat calls for a pink undercoat.
A Chinese calendar girl, naked, chaste and varnished,
simpers behind potplants like a jungle dawn.

Joy, local, it says in the phone-booth, with a number
next to it. Or *Petra*. Or *Out of Order*, and an arrow.
This last gives you pause, ten minutes, several weeks . . .
Delay deters the opportunist as much as doubt.

In an elementary deception, the name of the street
is taken from a country town, and when I get up
I find my education is back to haunt me: Dickens House,
Blake Court, Austen House, thirteen-storey giants.

Some Sunday mornings, blood trails down the street
from the night before. Stabbing, punch-up or nosebleed,
it's impossible to guess, but the drops fell thickly and easily
on the paving-stones, too many for the rules of hopscotch.

The roadway itself is reddish, the faded spongy brick
of the terrace is overpowered by the paintwork's
sweet dessert colours. They spoil it, but you understand
they are there as the sugar in tomato soup is there.

Clouds come over from the West, as always in England
the feeling that the sea is just beyond the next horizon:
a thick, Byzantine crucifix on a steep schoolhouse roof,
the slippery, ecclesiastical gleam of wet slate.

Dogs vet the garbage before the refuse collectors.
Brazen starlings and pigeons, 'flying rats', go over
what is left. Rough-necked, microcephalous, they have
too much white on their bodies, like calcium defectives.

The pigeons mate in full view: some preliminary billing,
then the male flutters his wings as though to break a
                                        fall . . .
They inhabit a ruined chiropodist's, coming and going freely
through broken windows into their cosy excremental hollow.

The old man in the vest in the old people's home
would willingly watch us all day. In their windows,
a kind of alcove, they keep wine bottles and candlesticks,
Torvill and Dean, a special occasion on ice.

The motor-mews has flat roofs of sandpaper or tarpaper.
One is terraced, like three descending trays of gravel.
Their skylights are angled towards the red East,
some are truncated pyramids, others whole glazed shacks.

Open House

Rawlplugs and polyfilla . . . the cheerful,
tamping thump of reggae through the floorboards,

the drawling vowel 'r' of Irish or Jamaican English
carrying easily through the heated, excitable air –

as though I lived in a museum without walls.

Snowdrops

(TEL 612 H)

The days are so dark they hardly count –
but they must have some marginal warmth after all,
for the drizzle of my night-breath turns to fog.

The window is opaque, a white mirror affirming
life goes on inside this damp lung of a room . . .
I have no perspective on the dotty winter clouds,

the pubic scrub of this street I am growing to hate,
with its false burglar alarms and sleeping policemen.
My exhalations blot out the familiar view.

I can tell without looking when your car draws up,
I know its tune as it reaches the end of its tether
and stops under the lamp-post, melodramatic and old-red,

the unwilling gift of your sainted grandmother
who disliked you and died suddenly on Friday.
'*Grand-merde*' you called her when you left sometimes

to go with her to visit your uncle in hospital,
lying there with irreversible brain damage
almost as long as I've lived here, after

falling downstairs drunk. You chat to him,
and imagine or fail to imagine that he responds
when you play him the recording of his greatest moment

when the horse he trained won the Derby.
I stay here and listen to sport on the radio,
a way of processing time to trial and outcome.

Someone brought me some cigarettes from America
called *Home Run*, and they frighten me half to death
in their innocuous vernal packaging, green and yellow.

Kif

The filter crumples – a cruel exhilaration
as the day's first cigarette draws to a close.
The optician's colours turn to a dizzy whiteness
in my solar plexus . . . With longing I speculate
on Heimito von Doderer's excursus on tobacco –
the pharmaceutical precision of the true scholar.

Disturbances

I go over to my window in South Cambridge,
where the Official Raving Loony Monster candidate
stands to poll half a per cent – the moral majority . . .

Below me, the idyllic lilac tree has scorched
to beehive, to beeswax, to *Bienenstich*, a spongy cack.
Voorman parks his purple car in its shade.

I picture him underneath it, his helter-skelter
fat man jeans halfway down, showing his anal cleft.
Though what would he be doing, face down like that?!

He's even more remote than I am, curtains drawn,
stopping the plug-hole with his hair-loss,
never a letter for him, a visit or a phone-call.

How is it, then, that in the featurelessness
of his Sundays he throws fits, shouting and swearing,
punching the walls, putting us in fear of our lives?

I'm so fearful and indecisive, all my life
has been in education, higher and higher education . . .
What future for the fly with his eye on the flypaper?

The house is breaking up, and still I'm hanging on here:
scaffolding and a skip at the door, smells of dust
and sawdust, the trepanation of the floorboards.

Between Bed and Wastepaper Basket

There hasn't been much to cheer about in three years
in this boxroom shaped like a loaf of bread,
the flimsy partitions of the servants' quarters,
high up in the drafty cranium of the house.

All things tend towards the yellow of unlove,
the tawny, moulting carpet where I am commemorated
by tea- and coffee-stains, by the round holes of furniture –
too much of it, and too long in the same place.

Here, we have been prepared for whatever comes next.
The dishonest, middle-aged anorexic has been moved on.
The radio-buff is now responsible for contact
in the cardboard huts of the British Antarctic Survey.

(His great antenna was demolished here one stormy night.)
The tiny American professor is looking for tenure.
On occasional passionate weekends, the vinegary
smell of cruel spermicide carried all before it.

Familiarity breeds mostly the fear of its loss.
In winter, the ice-flowers on the inside of the window
and the singing of the loose tap; in summer,
the thunderflies that came in and died on my books

like bits of misplaced newsprint . . . I seize the day
when you visited me here – the child's world in person:
gold shoes, grass skirt, sky blouse and tinted, cirrus hair.
We went outside. Everything in the garden was rosy.

Prefabs ran down the back of the Applied Psychology Unit.
Pigeons dilated. The flies were drowsy from eating
the water-lilies on the pond. A snake had taken care of
the frogs. Fuchsias pointed their toes like ballerinas.

My hand tried to cup your breast. You were jail-bait,
proposing a miraculous career as county wife
and parole officer. We failed to betray
whatever trust was placed in us.

Against Nature

Des Esseintes himself would have admired
her fastidiousness – anorexia, years in hospital –
as he gloated over his own peptone enemas . . .
Her horror is a purely physical matter.
If she had her way, it would all cease.

Like sticks of furniture swathed in sheets,
her limbs ghost about the place, longing for peace,
disuse. She walks fast to lose weight –
a blue streak, hoping for invisibility
behind '60s dyed hair and false eyelashes.

In a gesture of self-betrayal, she goes shopping:
powdered milk, Gitanes, cans of cat food
to placate Sappho, her black panther of a cat . . .
A Japanese lodger lived there for a while.
In his country, there are many centenarians –

rice, raw fish, and the subjugation of women
combine to promote longevity in the male.
A dietary expert, he drank as much beer
in an evening as a special *kobe* beef cow.
He never cleaned the bath, and left rich stains

in the lavatory bowl, like a dirty protest . . .
She has a boyfriend of sorts, weird, well-spoken,
Jesus-bearded. His childhood squints from one eye.
Something out of Dostoevsky, he wears only
navy blue – the colour of religious aspirants.

An anonymous depressive, he talks her into knots.
. . . Often, he isn't allowed in to see her.
Then his notes bristle on the doormat like fakirs,
her name on them in big block capitals,
widely spaced on the paranoid envelope . . .

Campaign Fever

We woke drugged and naked. Did our flowers
rob us and beat us over the head while we were asleep?
They were competing for the same air as us –
the thick, vegetable breath of under the eaves.

It seems like several days ago that I went
to see you to your train. A cuckoo called
and our vision drizzled, though the air was dry.
In a place I'd never noticed before, a low siren

was sounding alternate notes. I remembered
it had been going all night. Was it in distress?
I slept four times, and ate with the base,
groundless haste of someone eating alone.

Afterwards I smoked a cigarette and lay on my back
panting, as heavy and immobile as my own saliva.
The newspapers preyed on my mind. On the radio,
the National Front had five minutes to put their case.

The fiction of an all-white Albion, deludedness
and control, like my landlady's white-haired old bitch,
who confuses home with the world, pees just inside the door,
and shits trivially in a bend in the corridor.

Mr Thatcher made his pile by clearing railway lines
with sheep-dip (the millionaire's statutory one idea).
When he sold his shares, they grew neglected,
plants break out and reclaim the very pavements . . .

I think of you trundling across Middle England,
Peterborough, Leicester, Birmingham New Street –
the onetime marginals – up to your eyes in a vigorous,
delinquent haze of buttercups, milfoil and maple scrub.

PART 2: MY FATHER'S HOUSE

Day of Reckoning

When we drove across America, going West,
I tanned through the sandwich glass windscreen.
Though I was eight, and my legs weren't yet long
in their long pants, I could still sit in front –

your co-driver who couldn't spell you . . .
My jagged elbow stuck out of the right-hand window,
I kept a tough diary, owned a blunt knife,
and my mother sat in the back with the girls.

I can't remember if we talked, or if, even then,
you played the radio, but when I got tired
I huddled in my legroom in the Chevy Belair,
and watched the coloured stars under the dashboard . . .

I learned fractions from you in a single day,
multiplying and dividing. In Kingston, Ontario,
I had a cruel haircut. For you, it was a dry time –
in two years one short play about bankruptcy:

Let Them Down, Gently. There followed the great crash.

Mexico '66

The scene is so wrong I've lost you from it,
but you were right there with us as we crept down to earth
from Mexico City, five of us cooped up, all present
and correct. The train stopped for a chicken,

or if the line was too crooked or too straight,
or for no reason at all. Three days . . . 'Earth' was El Paso,
a T-bone steak, the re-union with your purple Chevy,
marooned for weeks in the *al fresco* border car-park.

And then the empty highways of Arizona and New Mexico
in the impatient night, the neon more blue than white
– a soft, blinking, blissful violet, better than day –
and we made 'Frisco in the twinkling of an eye . . .

The city was building for its Olympics,
but surely it would never be ready. Without meat and water,
it was like America gone bad, America built on toxicity:
chilli dogs, alcohol, sugar and chocolate.

You had to shave in treacly Coke or tequila!
A wave unpeeled a bill of skin from my back.
Young men swallow-dived into shallows for a few dollars.
On the Pacific, on the golden sand, they turned

the turtles and slit them, still living, from their shells.
Madly, the *Estrella d'Oro* buses shot the hairpin bends
as though the cliffs silhouetted in the corrupt sunsets
were cut paper. Giddy and beside myself with nitrogen,

I acquiesced in all our deaths . . . I sorrowed
for the boy with the prophetic, Mexico-patterned pyjamas;
who haggled, a nervous *gringo*, for a Christmas balloon;
and built himself a future as a chicken farmer, counting

how many hens he might get from the three-day-old chicks,
egg-yolk yellow, dirt-cheap, milling about by the side of the
road
in cardboard crates, cardboard coffins . . . And I mourned his
father,
who had told him about import restrictions and fowl-pest.

The Machine That Cried

'Il n'y a pas de détail' – Paul Valéry

When I learned that my parents were returning
to Germany, and that I was to be jettisoned,
I gave a sudden lurch into infancy and Englishness.
Carpets again loomed large in my world: I sought out
their fabric and warmth, where there was nowhere to fall . . .

I took up jigsaw puzzles, read mystical cricket thrillers
passing all understanding, even collected toy soldiers
and killed them with matchsticks fired from the World War
                                                        One
field-guns I bought from Peter Oborn down the road
– he must have had something German, with that name –

who lived alone with his mother, like a man . . .
My classmates were equipped with sexual insults
for the foaming lace of the English women playing
                                                Wimbledon,
but I watched them blandly on our rented set
behind drawn curtains, without ever getting the point.

My building-projects were as ambitious as the Tower of
                                                        Babel.
Something automotive of my construction limped across the
                                                        floor
to no purpose, only lugging its heavy battery.
Was there perhaps some future for Christiaan Barnard,
or the electric car, a milk-float groaning like a sacred heart?

I imagined Moog as von Moog, a mad German scientist.
His synthesizer was supposed to be the last word in
                                        versatility,
but when I first heard it on Chicory Tip's
Son of my Father, it was just a unisono metallic drone,
five notes, as inhibited and pleonastic as the title.

My father bought a gramophone, a black box,
and played late Beethoven on it, which my mother was always
to associate with her miscarriage of that year.
I was forever carrying it up to my room,
and quietly playing through my infant collection of singles,

Led Zeppelin, The Tremoloes, *My Sweet Lord* . . .
The drums cut like a scalpel across the other instruments.
Sometimes the turntable rotated slowly, then everything
went flat, and I thought how with a little more care
it could have been all right. There again, so many things

were undependable . . . My first-ever British accent wavered
between Pakistani and Welsh. I called *Bruce's* record shop
just for someone to talk to. He said, 'Certainly, Madam.'
Weeks later, it was 'Yes sir, you can bring your children.'
It seemed I had engineered my own birth in the new country.

My Father's House Has Many Mansions

Who could have said we belonged together,
my father and my self, out walking, our hands held
behind our backs in the way Goethe recommended?

Our heavy glances tipped us forward – the future,
a wedge of pavement with our shoes in it . . .
In your case, beige, stacked, echoing clogs;

and mine, the internationally scruffy tennis shoes –
seen but not heard – of the protest movement.
My mother shook her head at us from the window.

I was taller and faster but more considerate:
tense, overgrown, there on sufferance, I slowed down
and stooped for you. I wanted to share your life.

Live with you in your half-house in Ljubljana,
your second address: talk and read books;
meet your girl-friends, short-haired, dark, oral;

go shopping with cheap red money in the supermarket;
share the ants in the kitchen, the unfurnished rooms,
the fallible winter plumbing. Family was abasement

and obligation . . . The three steps to your door
were three steps to heaven. But there were only visits.
At a party for your students – my initiation! –

I ceremoniously downed a leather glass of *slivovica*.
But then nothing. I wanted your mixture of resentment
and pride in me expanded to the offer of equality.

Is the destination of paternity only advice . . . ?
In their ecstasy of growth, the bushes along the drive
scratch your bodywork, dislocate your wing-mirror.

Every year, the heraldic plum-tree in your garden
surprises you with its small, rotten fruit.

Bärli

Your salami breath tyrannized the bedroom
where you slept on the left, my mother, tidily,
on the right. I could cut the atmosphere with a knife:

the enthusiasm for spice, rawness, vigour,
in the choppy air. It was like your signature,
a rapid scrawl from the side of your pen –

individual, overwhelming, impossible –
a black Greek energy that cramped itself into
affectionate diminutives, *Dein Vati*, or *Papi*.

At forty, you had your tonsils out, child's play
with Little Bear nuns, Ursulines for nurses.
Hours after the operation, you called home . . .

humbled and impatient, you could only croak.
I shivered at your weakness – the faint breeze
that blew through you and formed words.

Lighting Out

Business, independence, a man alone, travelling –
I was on your territory. Though what I represented
was not myself, but a lawnmower manufacturer,
whipping round the green belts in Northern Germany.

Hardly your line, then – that would have been
a tour of radio stations, or public readings –
but once I swanned off to mercantile Lübeck, and saw
Thomas Mann's ugly Nobel plaque, and the twin towers

on fifty-mark banknotes. And I coincided
with the publication of your firstborn, *The Denunciation*.
I proudly bought a copy on my expenses, giving you
your first royalties on twenty-odd years of my life . . .

But being a salesman was dispiriting work. I ran myself
like an organization, held out the prospect of bonuses,
wondered which of the tiny, sad, colourful bottles
in my freezing minibar I would crack next.

The Means of Production

Like a man pleading for his life,
you put novels between yourself
and your pursuers – Atalanta,
always one step ahead of the game.

You gave me a copy of your second
with the dedication: *Michael,*
something else for you to read.
Your disparaging imperative

was too much resented for obedience . . .
You were a late starter at fiction,
but for ten years now, your family
has been kept at arm's length.

– We are as the warts on your elbows,
scratched into submission, but always
recrudescent. You call each of us
child, your wife and four children,

three of them grown-up. You have
the biblical manner: the indulgent patriarch,
his abused, endless patience; smiling
the absent smile of inattention . . .

Everything you need is at your desk:
glue-stained typewriter, match-sticks,
unravelled paper-clips – *Struwwelpeter* props!
With your big work-scissors, you snipe

at your nails, making the sparks fly.
The radio updates its bulletins
every hour, guarding you against surprises.
The living breath of the contemporary . . .

Once, you acceded to conversation,
got up to put on your black armband
and took your blood-pressure, as though
in the presence of an unacceptable risk.

Vortex

Where was our high-water mark? Was it the glorious
oriental scimitar in the Metropolitan Museum
in New York? Nothing for a pussyfooting shake-hands grip:
your hand had to be a fist already to hold it . . .
I wondered why the jewels were all clustered
on scabbard and hilt and basketed hand-guard,
why there were none on the sword itself.
I could only guess that the blade leapt out
to protect them, like a strong father his family.

– Or next door, where, as the guide explained,
there was a deity in the ceiling, who would shower
genius or intellect or eyewash on those beneath?
And straightaway, to my fierce embarrassment,
you pushed me under it, an un-European moment –
though I tried also to relish the shiver of limelight.

– Or was it more even, less clinching, the many years
I used the basin after you had shaved in it?
It was my duty to shave the basin, rinsing
the circle of hairs from its concave enamel face
till it was as smooth as yours . . . I was almost there,
on the periphery of manhood, but I didn't have your gear:
the stiff brush of real badger (or was it beaver?);
the reserved cake of shaving soap; the safety razor
that opened like Aladdin's cave when I twirled the handle.
. . . That movement became an escape mechanism:
I was an orphan, a street Arab, waiting for you
in international lounges, at the foot of skyscrapers;
entertaining myself with the sprinkler nozzles
secreted in the ceiling, whirling dervishes
sniffing out smoke, in a state of permanent readiness;
or with the sprung, centrifugal, stainless ashtrays
that have since emancipated me, like the razors
– cheapskate, disposable, no moving parts –
I now use myself . . . The water drains away, laughing.
I light up, a new man.

Withdrawn from Circulation

My window gave on to a street-corner where the air currents
(*Berliner Luft*!) were of such bewildering complexity
that the snow, discouraged, fell back up the sky . . .

It stayed shut, and I sweated in the central heat
as I sweated in my pyjamas at night, snug as a worm
in my slithery tapering orange-and-green sleeping bag.

For a whole month, the one soiled bedsheet
was supposed to knit together, to join in matrimony
the shiny blue tripartite mattress, borrowed or looted

from a ruined office, but good as new.
Small wonder I hugged it in sleep! On the floor
lay the door that was to have made me a table.

It was said there was nothing between here and Siberia –
except Poland – but indoors was the tropics.
I was eighteen, and frittering away.

I picked up just enough politics to frighten my mother,
and the slick, witless phrases I used about girls
were a mixture of my father's and those I remembered

from *Mädchen* or *Bravo* . . . Nothing quite touched me.
I put on weight, smoked Players and read Dickens
for anchorage and solidity. Come the autumn,

I was going to Cambridge. A few doors down
was the cellar where the RAF kept the Berlin Senator
they had kidnapped and were holding to ransom.

From time to time, his picture appeared
in the newspapers, authenticated by other newspapers
in the picture with him. He was news that stayed news.

Giro Account

Out of the pornographic cinema at the station,
with the fast clock and the continuous programme,
then past the French sweet-stall, the naturist magazines

and the cretin at the lottery ticket-office
– *das schnelle Glück*: a quick buck or fuck –
and into the night train to Berlin . . .

It was sealed and non-stop, but East German border guards
woke us up so they could give us our transit visas,
and then it was early on Sunday, and I walked

out of *Berlin-Zoo* in my father's lion coat,
his suitcase in one hand and his bag in the other.
I was nineteen and a remittance man,

embarked on a delirium of self-sufficiency,
surprised that it was possible to live like a bird:
to stay in a hotel, to eat in restaurants,

and draw my father's money from a giro account.
At the end of my feeding-tube, I didn't realize
that to stay anywhere on the earth's surface is to bleed:

money, attention, effort . . . It was no problem.
I avoided my companions – the cold young man
with the Inca cap, the weak heart and the blue face,

his obese, scatologically-brained sister – and stared
incessantly at a Peruvian woman in a night-club.
There was a girl who one day told me she'd become engaged.

The motherly hotel manageress gave me the rolls
left over from my breakfast for the rest of the day.
Once, she gave me my father on the telephone.

I asked him about his conference, but he wanted
something else: to have me at the end of a telephone
line, an alibi, proof of my harmlessness –

he had become jealous of a spivvy young Englishman . . .
There was no crime, no conference, maybe no Englishman:
only my father, his son and his new novel plot.

And the Teeth of the Children Are Set on Edge

It's the twenty-fifth and I'm twenty-five. Already,
I've spent a half-life cornered, listening to you.
When I come upstairs from my bedroom in the cellar,
I can see you've been waiting for me, preparing yourself.
There are few preliminaries. The words have been
gathering inside you, now they are ready to come out.
The point of tears is an hour away. You want to talk.
'He says, "I've done better with my life than you.
I've won my prizes, what have you got to show?"
We are competing tombstones, he puts me in the shade.
. . . Everything reaches him only through his egotism.
Talking to a female colleague, he says he is blessed
with a poor memory. In the morning he gets up
and revises, as though it were someone else's work.
She does her writing in the daytime, and in the evening
reads it to her husband. Mine finds that incomprehensible:
participation, involvement, sharing! She replies
that she is too close to it, she has no objectivity,
so now my husband goes around saying, "This person
knows *my* work by heart . . ." You should ask more of him,
otherwise it all goes on this Dulcinea of his.
Does he expect me to believe he crossed the Alps that time?
I know they stayed in Salzburg. With a horrible smile,
he told me he had been spoiled . . . His hotel bills
are mountainous, there are telegram receipts, the lot.
One day he went to buy himself a coat, and came back
with two parcels, which we weren't allowed to go near.
Think of them in their *partner-look* . . . I remember
typing his early confessional novel, and going away
to cry after each few pages . . .'
                                        My little sister
meanders past in unwashed denim, the new kid in town.
Black-eyed Susie, she's eight but she thinks she's fifteen.

Birds of Passage

'The slash of rain. Outside the window, blackbirds
shoot around like dark clouds in the sycamore.
It is meat and drink to them. Between its leaves,
the sky is silver paper, the end of their world . . .

I stare away. I don't want to watch the circus
of my husband's homecoming, a bankrupt show
of defensiveness, guilt and irritability . . .
Two routes in his head, two itineraries, two women.'

Errant

In your absence, it's up to me to be the man of the house,
and listen to the late news with my mother. And afterwards,
Euro Radio Reise Rufe, private calamities available to a few
people
on top of the global ones. Missing persons, a sudden illness –
or any dramatic *good* news? We both think the same thing:
Gert Hofmann, travelling in Yugoslavia in a silver Audi 100 . . .
The appointment you kept for twelve years (even though
it was only provisional and intended for a younger man
anyway)
ended this summer, and we have your disestablished
household
and a late rent demand forwarded here to prove it.
With every instalment of property, my mother seemed
to be nearer to reclaiming you: books, furniture,
your favoured avant-garde lamps – feminine abstracts! . . .

Being away was a drug. Your family safely parked
across the border – your departure advanced from week to
week –
you set off, newly bathed, appetizing, dressed in white,
cutting the corners of the mountain passes in your messianic
car!
Twelve years with a double life as a part-time bachelor!
The end of the pretext didn't mean the end of the place.
With no more reason to be there, you manufacture a quarrel
and leave on a careful impulse. I've had only three days with
you.
They didn't add up to much. Once more, you proved not to be
the decrepit old man I double-take at the station.

But the beaverish wrinkles of feeding or disdain or both
have deepened beside your nose and mouth. Under your
eyes,
clarified by balloon spectacles, I see bleak anal pleats.

Once, you offered me your clippings file – the human touch!
What next: a translator's essays, a printed interview?
This time, there's a new string to the bow of your activities.
Dressed in grey from top to toe, with a grey beard, grey face,
grey felt country hat, you disappear into the garden with
a shovel
like a one-man death squad. The caramel-coloured plain-and-
purl slugs
have to learn that speed kills, relatively speaking.
It's your one concession to gardening . . . For a long time,
you thought of having a work-hut put up in the garden –
the satellite existence of the writer made flesh.
You could turn it round to be in the sun . . . It's a standard
dream
that maybe you still have, though imperceptibly it's become
absurd, like having a pleasant evening at home.

Catechism

My father peers into the lit sitting-room
and says, 'Are you here?' . . . Yes, I am,
in one of his cloudy white leather armchairs,
with one foot not too disrespectfully on the table,
reading Horváth's *Godless Youth*. Without another word,
he goes out again, baffling and incommunicable,
the invisible man, dampening any speculation.

My Father at Fifty

Your mysterious economy blows the buttons
off your shirts, and permits overdrafts
at several foreign banks. – It must cost the earth.

Once I thought of you virtually as a savage,
atavistic, well-aligned, without frailties.
A man of strong appetites, governed by instinct.

You never cleaned your teeth, but they were perfect anyway
from a diet of undercooked meat; you gnawed the bones;
anything sweet you considered frivolous.

Your marvellous, single-minded régime, kept up
for years, of getting up at four or five,
and writing a few pages 'on an empty stomach',

before exposing yourself to words – whether
on the radio, in books or newspapers,
or just your own from the day before . . .

Things are different now. Your male discriminations
– meat and work – have lost their edge.
Your teeth are filled, an omnivorous sign.

Wherever you are, there is a barrage of noise:
your difficult breathing, or the blaring radio –
as thoughtless and necessary as breathing.

You have gone to seed like Third World dictators,
fat heads of state suffering horribly
from Western diseases whose name is Legion . . .

Your concentration is gone: every twenty minutes,
you go to the kitchen, or you call your wife
over some trifle. Bad-tempered and irritable,

you sedate yourself to save the energy
of an outburst. Your kidneys hurt, there is even
a red band of eczema starring your chest.

Your beard – the friend of the writer who doesn't smoke –
is shot with white . . . A Christmas card arrives
to ask why you don't have any grandchildren.

Author, Author

'verba volant, scripta manent'

Can this be all that remains – two or three weeks a year,
sitting at the opposite end of the dinner table from my
                                              father?

To listen to his breathing, more snorting than breathing,
puffing out air through his nose during mouthfuls,

chewing loudly with open mouth, without enjoyment,
uninhibited, inhibiting, his only talk, talk of food?

And to watch myself watching him, fastidious and disloyal,
feeling my muscles through my shirt – an open knife!

(My own part of the conversation, thin, witty, inaudible,
as though I'd spoken in asides for twenty-five years.)

To come back to him unannounced, at regular intervals,
one of two or three unselfsufficient, cryptic,

grown-up strangers he has fathered, and see again
his small silver mouth in his great grizzled face,

head and stomach grown to childlike proportions,
supported on his unchanging, teenager's legs . . .

To come upon by chance, while emptying the dustbin,
the ripped, glittery foil-wrapping of his heart-medicines,

multiplication times-tables of empty capsules,
dosages like police ammunition in a civil disturbance,

bought for cash over the counter and taken according to
need –
like his sudden peremptory thirst for a quart of milk.

If sex is nostalgia for sex, and food nostalgia for food,
his can't be – what did a child of the War get to eat

that he would want to go on eating, and to share?
Standing in the road as the American trucks rolled by:

chewing-gum, cigarettes, canned herrings, a kick in the
teeth.
(The way it is with dogs, and their first puppy nourishment:

potato-peelings, or my maternal grandmother in East
Germany,
and Chéri, her gay dog – pampered, shy, neurotic Chéri,

corrupted by affection, his anal glands spoiling with
virginity –
she feeds him heart and rice, the only cooking she ever
does.) . . .

After the age of fifty, a sudden flowering, half a dozen
novels
in as many years – dialogue by other means: his main
characters

maniacs, compulsive, virtuoso talkers, talkers for dear life,
talkers in soliloquies, notebooks, tape-recordings, last
wills . . .

Hear him on the telephone, an overloud, forced bonhomie,
standing feet crossed, and one punishing the other for
lying,

woken up once at midnight by a drunken critic
with his girl-friend hanging on the extension –

her sweet name not a name at all, but a blandishment –
finishing with promises, and his vestigial phrase of English

after ten years in England, '*Bye, bye.*' Then going off to pee,
like the boys at my boarding-school after fire-practice . . .

Till that time, I had a worshipful proximity with him,
companionable and idolatrous. If my nose wasn't hooked,

my hair not black and straight, my frame too long,
my fingers not squat and powerful, fitting the typewriter keys,

then it was my mother's fault, her dilution, her adulteration.
Home from England, I landed on a checkered pattern

of unwillingness and miserable advice. Not to take drugs,
not to treat my face with vinegar or lemon-juice,

to make influential friends, and not to consort with others.
And, on interesting subjects, either a silence

or the interviewee's too-rapid turning to his own
                                        experience . . .
Perplexed, wounded, without confidence, I left him to
                                            himself,

first going round the block on a small-wheeled bicycle
in one of his leather jackets, like an elderly terror;

or, now, on walks with my mother in the shitty park
among the burghers: his duffle-coat in the zoo of democracy.

A performance, like everything else . . . What's the point?
He wants only his car and his typewriter and his Magic
                                                    Marker.

Every action he divides into small stages, every traffic light
on the way home, and each one he punctuates with a
                                        crucified 'So.'

I ask myself what sort of consummation is available?
Fight; talk literature and politics; get drunk together?

Kiss him goodnight, as though half my life had never
                                        happened?

Fine Adjustments

By now, it is almost my father's arm,
a man's arm, that lifts the cigarettes to my mouth
numbed by smoke and raw onions and chocolate milk.

I need calm, something to tranquillize me
after the sudden storm between us that left me shaking,
and with sticky palms . . . It only happens here,

where I blurt in German, dissatisfied and unproficient
amid the material exhilaration of abstract furniture,
a new car on the Autobahn, electric pylons walking

through the erasures in the Bayrischer Wald . . .
Once before, I left some lines of Joseph Roth
bleeding on your desk: '*I had no father – that is,*

I never knew my father – but Zipper had one.
That made my friend seem quite privileged,
as though he had a parrot or a St Bernard.'

All at once, my nature as a child hits me.
I was a moving particle, like the skidding lights
in a film-still. Provoking and of no account,

I kept up a constant rearguard action, jibing,
commenting, sermonizing. 'Why did God give me a voice,'
I asked, 'if you always keep the radio on?'

It was a fugitive childhood. Aged four, I was chased
round and round the table by my father, who fell
and broke his arm he was going to raise against me.

Digital Recordings

Everything feels soft to my hands useless with cold
in this high-style country cottage, a retreat
for painters and musicians in summer. I put them up

and feel my father's head, his thinning, pliant hair
and embayed temples – there to threaten or impress women,
I once read, with the frontal bone of intellect . . .

The central heating clicks on, and the warm air
shoots straight up into the triangular apex of the studio,
against twenty feet of northlight, now darkness and fog.

I've no reason to believe there's anything below me –
the presumed foundations, whichever of God's creatures
left their prints in the snow and didn't turn aside,

the taped felt undercarpet worn down by unknowns
and by the organist of Chelmsford Cathedral –
but I bring into it Trevor from downstairs,

security guard at HMV and abject night-time guitarist,
tapping his foot into a pile of blankets,
black-and-blue notes whimpering through the floor . . .

My fingers whiten as they bunch themselves
to grip my father's pen. Silver and surgically thin,
taken in error, its ink is thicker than blood.

Old Firm

Father, the winter bird writes bird's nest soup –
a frail, disciplined structure, spun from its spittle
with bits of straw and dirt, then boiled with beaten eggs . . .
It kept us fed till we were big enough to leave the nest.

We walked, *à trois*, to the end of the road, for my bus
to Riem, and the plane to Gatwick, seemingly
chartered by the *Bierfest* . . . A sudden thunderstorm
turned us into a family group: mother under her umbrella,

you hiding in a phone-box, kindly holding the door open,
and me, giving no protection, and pretending
not to seek any either, wet and deserting and plastered,
like the hair making itself scarce on your bad head . . .

That morning you played me an interview you gave in French,
a language you hadn't spoken in my lifetime,
literally not since my birth, when you'd been in Toulouse,
on French leave . . . Now, we joked about it –

you were easier to understand than the interviewer!
Who else understood? Your edgy, defeated laugh?
The modest, unhopeful evangelism of your final appeal
to the people of Montreal not to stop reading?